Tuning In

A World of Sport can be read from beginn
be more appropriate to read selected sect
take account of this.

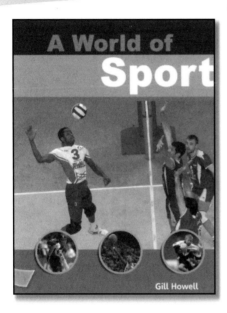

The front cover

Read the title. Why do you think it is called 'A World of Sport'?

Speaking and Listening

What sports do you expect to read about?

The back cover

Read the blurb to find out more.

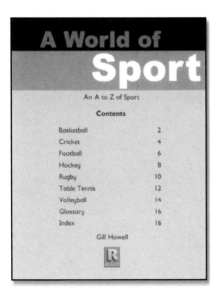

Contents

Flick through the pages. What do you see at the top of each page?

Read the list of contents. What have you noticed about the list?

Turn to the index on page 16. How many times is 'China' mentioned in the text?

Think of a question, beginning with 'How', 'What', or 'Which' to ask about China.

Turn to page 12. Scan the text to find 'China'. Read the sentence before and after and see if you can answer the question.

READ

Read pages 2 and 3

Purpose: to find out where basketball is played.

EXPLORE

Pause at page 3

What are the rules for basketball?

Speaking and Listening

Think of a question about the text, beginning with 'Who' or 'How' that you could ask the group.

Basketball

Two teams of five people play in a basketball match. They throw or bounce the ball to each other. Kicking it is not allowed, but the players can move with the ball. A goal is scored by throwing the ball into a **basket**.

Basketball is popular in the USA and Russia. In the 2004 Olympics, the Americans won the gold medal and the Russians took the bronze.

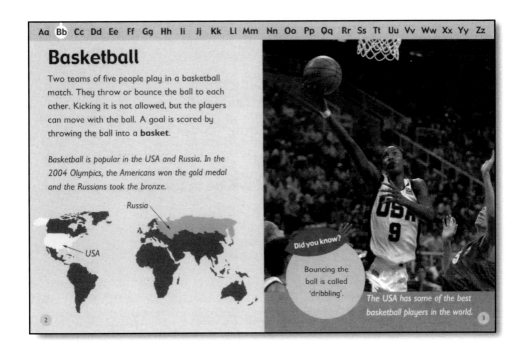

Russia

USA

Did you know?

Bouncing the ball is called 'dribbling'.

The USA has some of the best basketball players in the world.

2

3

READ

Read pages 4 and 5

Purpose: to think of a question about the text, beginning with 'Who', 'What' or 'How' that you could ask the group.

EXPLORE

Pause at page 5

Find the answers to the questions in the text.

Speaking and Listening

What are the words that will be in the glossary?

How are they explained?

Cricket

Cricket is played with a bat, ball and two sets of posts called **wickets**. The **bowler** tries to knock down the wicket behind the batsman. The batsman tries to hit the ball and run to the second wicket near the bowler.

Cricket is one of the most popular sports in England and Pakistan. In 1992, Pakistan won the World Cup when they beat England.

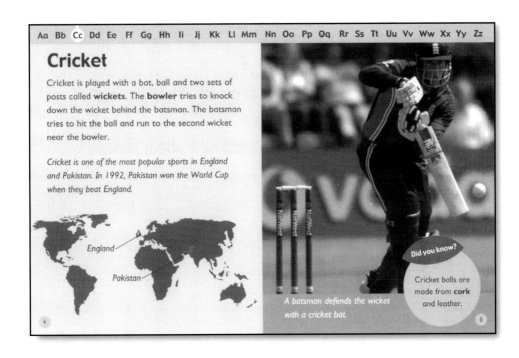

England

Pakistan

A batsman defends the wicket with a cricket bat.

Did you know?

Cricket balls are made from **cork** and leather.

READ

Read pages 6 and 7

Purpose: to find one fact that you didn't know before.

EXPLORE

Pause at page 7

Why do you think football is such a popular game?

Speaking and Listening

Have you found out anything new about football by reading these pages?

Football

There are 11 players in a football team. Players score goals by kicking the ball into a net. A goalkeeper on each side tries to stop the ball going into the net. The goalkeeper is the only player that can use his hands.

Football is the world's most popular sport. It is played in over 160 countries. It was probably introduced to England by the Romans.

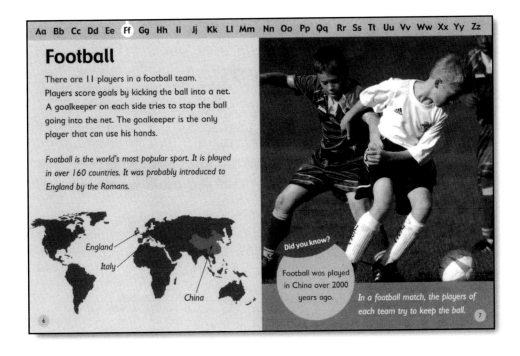

England

Italy

China

Did you know?

Football was played in China over 2000 years ago.

In a football match, the players of each team try to keep the ball.

6

7

7

READ

Read pages 8 and 9

Purpose: to find out the similarities between hockey and football.

EXPLORE

Pause at page 9

Which is the oldest game, hockey or football?

Speaking and Listening

Think of a question about the text, beginning with 'Where', 'What' or 'How' that you could ask the group.

Tricky words (page 9):
The word 'Egyptian' may be beyond the children's word recognition skills. Tell this word to the children.

The word 'tomb' may also want to be discussed as a tricky word.

Hockey

Hockey players use sticks to knock a ball, called a 'puck', into the goal. There are two goal nets on a hockey pitch – one for each side. Each goal counts as one point. There are 11 players in a team. Players wear shin pads to protect their legs.

Hockey is a popular game in India and Pakistan. It has been played for hundreds of years.

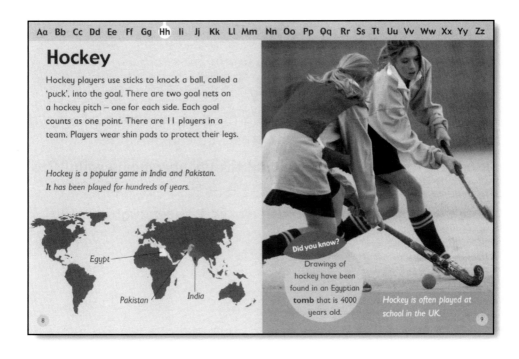

Egypt

Pakistan

India

Did you know?

Drawings of hockey have been found in an Egyptian **tomb** that is 4000 years old.

Hockey is often played at school in the UK.

8

9

READ

Read pages 10 and 11

Purpose: to find the differences between rugby and football.

EXPLORE

Pause at page 11

How did rugby get its name?

Speaking and Listening

Think of a question about the text, beginning with 'Who', 'What' or 'How' that you could ask the group.

Can you name two differences between rugby and football?

Rugby

In rugby, players can throw and kick the ball. They can run with the ball too. Rugby balls are **oval**. Players score points by touching the ground with the ball between two lines. The two lines are found at each end of the pitch.

Many people play rugby in the UK and France. There is a competition between France, England, Scotland, Ireland, Italy and Wales every year.

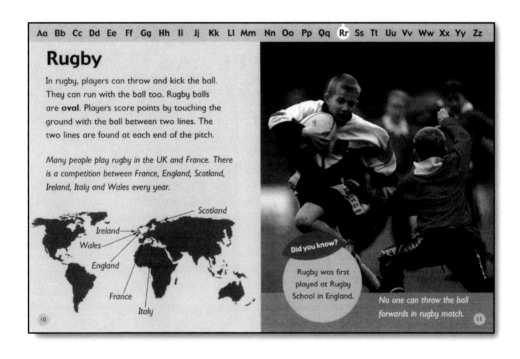

Scotland
Ireland
Wales
England
France
Italy

Did you know?

Rugby was first played at Rugby School in England.

No one can throw the ball forwards in rugby match.

10

11

11

READ

Read pages 12 and 13

Purpose: to find out which countries play table tennis.

EXPLORE

Pause at page 13

Which sport is older, football or table tennis?

Speaking and Listening

Think of a question about the text, beginning with 'Where', 'What' or 'How' that you could ask the group.

Tricky word (page 13):
The word 'soldiers' may be beyond the children's word recognition skills. Tell this word to the children.

Table Tennis

Table tennis is often called 'ping-pong'. Players hit a small ball over a net on top of a table, using a bat. These bats are sometimes called paddles.

Many people enjoy playing table tennis in China and Brazil. More than 100 countries take part in the world championships.

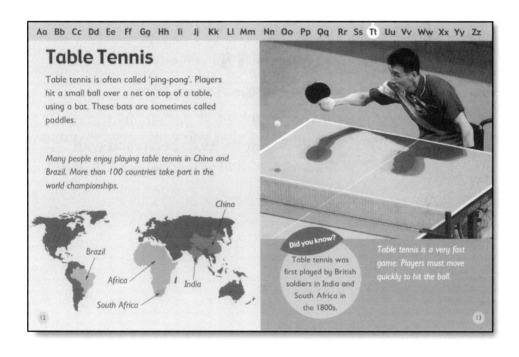

China

Brazil

Africa

India

South Africa

Did you know?
Table tennis was first played by British soldiers in India and South Africa in the 1800s.

Table tennis is a very fast game. Players must move quickly to hit the ball.

12

13

13

READ

Read pages 14 and 15

Purpose: to find out how to play volleyball.

EXPLORE

Pause at page 15

Which country does volleyball come from?

Speaking and Listening

Think of a question about the text, beginning with 'Where', 'What' or 'How' that you could ask the group.

Volleyball

There are six players on a volleyball team.
Players hit the ball over a high net with their
hands. If the ball touches the ground on the other
side of the net, the player scores a point. Players
hit the ball using either the palm or the side of
their hand.

Volleyball is a popular sport in Argentina and Greece.

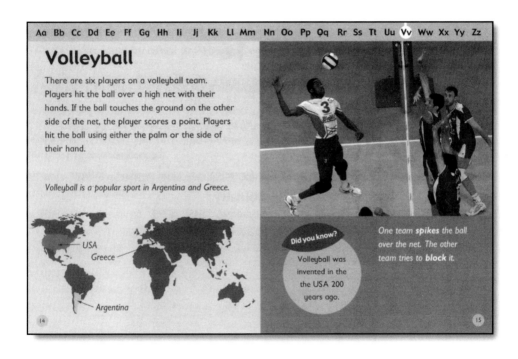

USA
Greece

Argentina

Did you know?

Volleyball was
invented in the
the USA 200
years ago.

One team **spikes** the ball
over the net. The other
team tries to **block** it.

14

15

READ

Read page 16

Purpose: to check the meanings of words in the glossary.

to use an index.

EXPLORE

Pause at page 16

Did you look up the meanings of all the words in bold type in the text?

Which countries are mentioned more than once in the index?

Look on the pages for England, Italy and Egypt. What does the text say about each country?

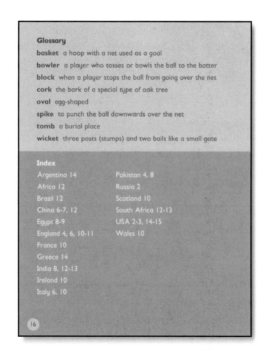

Glossary

basket a hoop with a net used as a goal

bowler a player who tosses or bowls the ball to the batter

block when a player stops the ball from going over the net

cork the bark of a special type of oak tree

oval egg-shaped

spike to punch the ball downwards over the net

tomb a burial place

wicket three posts (stumps) and two bails like a small gate

Index

Argentina 14   Pakistan 4, 8

Africa 12   Russia 2

Brazil 12   Scotland 10

China 6-7, 12   South Africa 12-13

Egypt 8-9   USA 2-3, 14-15

England 4, 6, 10-11   Wales 10

France 10

Greece 14

India 8, 12-13

Ireland 10

Italy 6, 10

16